SKULLS & ANATOMY

COPYRIGHT FREE VINTAGE ILLUSTRATIONS FOR ARTISTS AND DESIGNERS

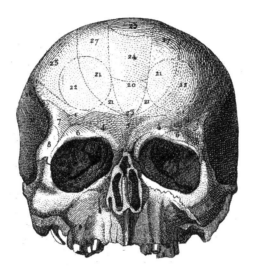

DOWNLOAD YOUR FILES

TO DOWNLOAD YOUR FILES FOLLOW THE LINK AND ENTER YOUR

UNIQUE ONE-TIME PASSWORD

VAULTEDITIONS.COM/SAA

UNIQUE PASSWORD: wxy74dt3

Vault Editions' team of designers and illustrators have spent a lifetime hunting and restoring vintage woodcuts and engravings from around the world to use to create amazing artwork. Now, we are opening the vault of our archives to the public.

SKULLS & ANATOMY

COPYRIGHT FREE VINTAGE ILLUSTRATIONS FOR ARTISTS AND DESIGNERS

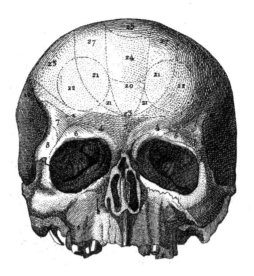

Skulls & Anatomy, Copyright Free Vintage Illustrations for Artists & Designers is a collection of 180 high quality, digitised, anatomical drawings for use in personal or commercial creative projects. This is an essential resource to take your art and design to the next level and give you a competitive advantage over your peers.

Within this collection, you will find rare, high-quality images carefully curated by our team of professional artists and designers who have used this imagery to create a range of projects, from gig-posters to identity design. We have carefully restored the artwork and provided a download link within the publication where you will locate high-resolution files in JPEG format as well as TIFF files with backgrounds removed to speed up your workflow. By collaging multiple images together, you can create impressive and dynamic designs in minutes that will impress both your clients and peers, no matter what your skill level is.

We hope we can provide a useful resource for you and your creative practice, if you have any feedback about our collection or particular topics you would like to suggest for future editions, we would love to hear from you. You can contact us via info@vaulteditions.com

We look forward to seeing the work you have created; please join us on Instagram at @VaultEditions.

ISBN: 978-0-6480497-6-0

A

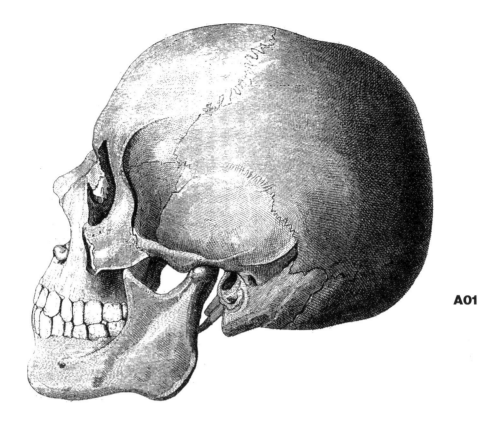

A01

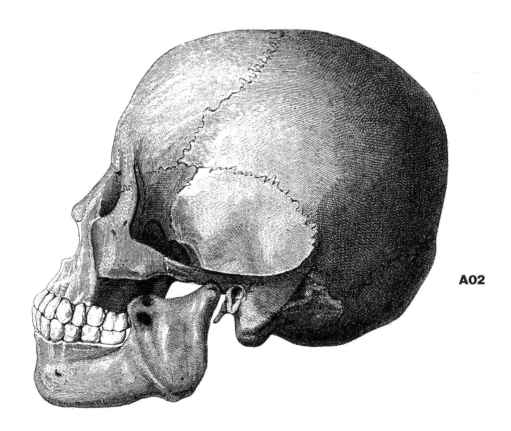

A02

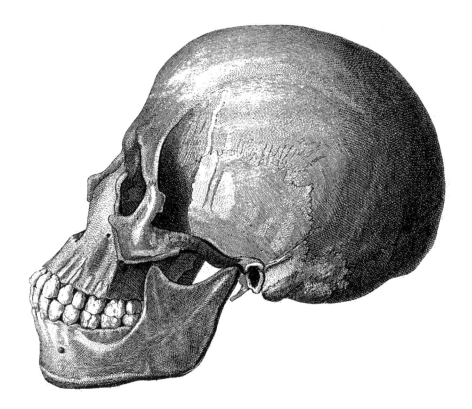

A03

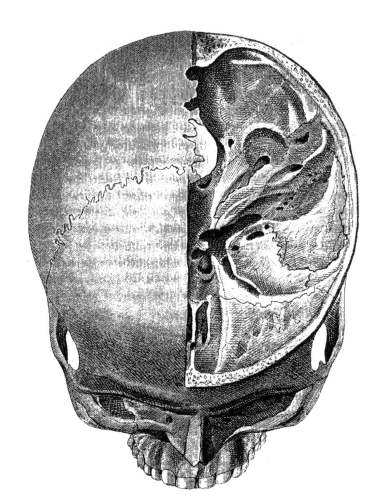

A04

A

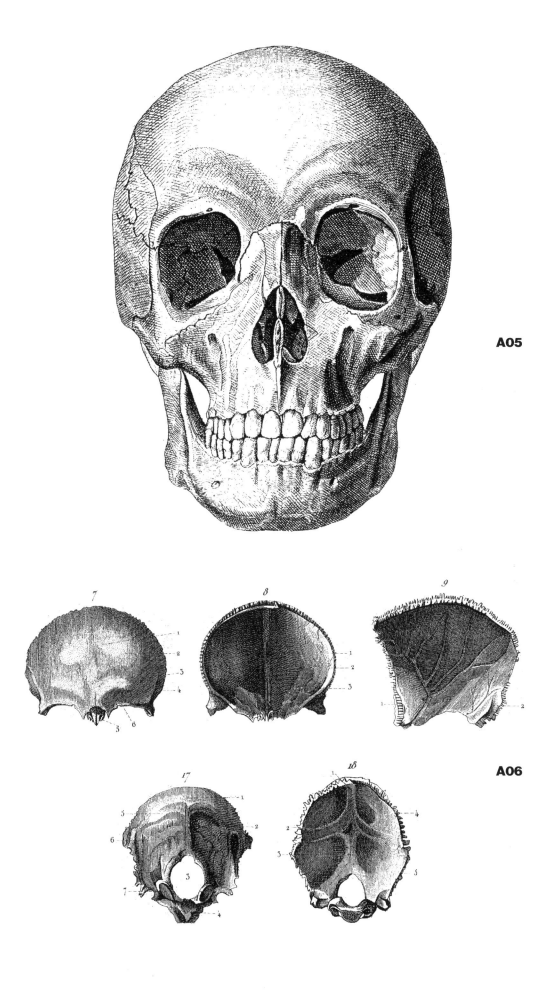

A05

A06

A

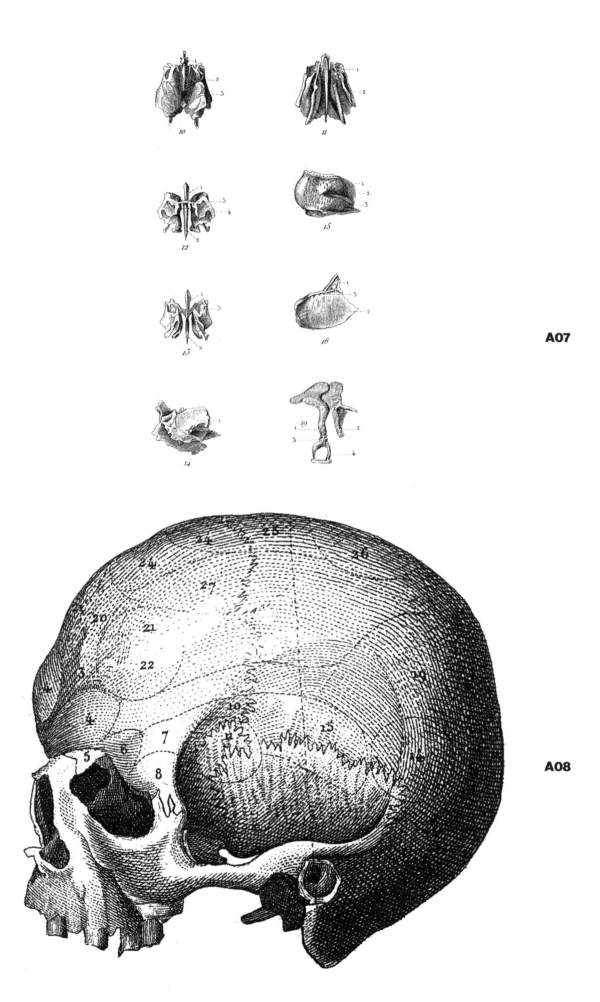

A07

A08

A

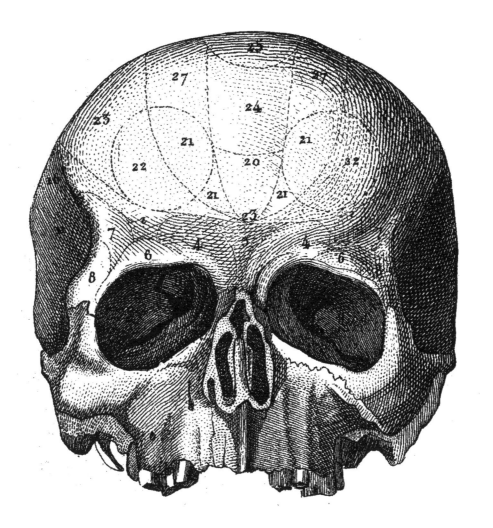

A09

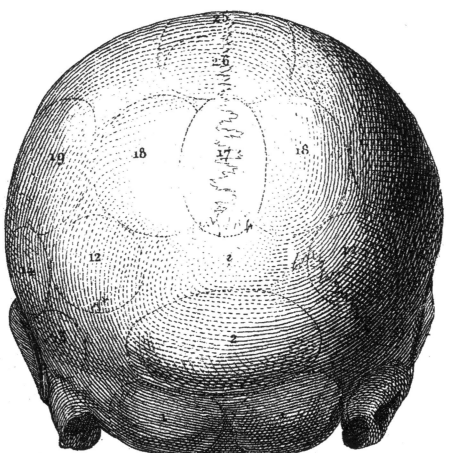

A10

A

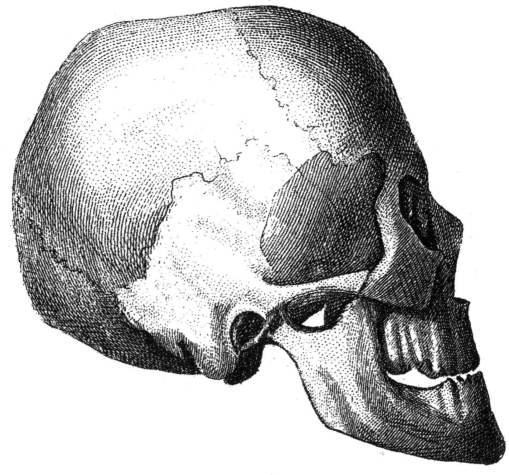

A11

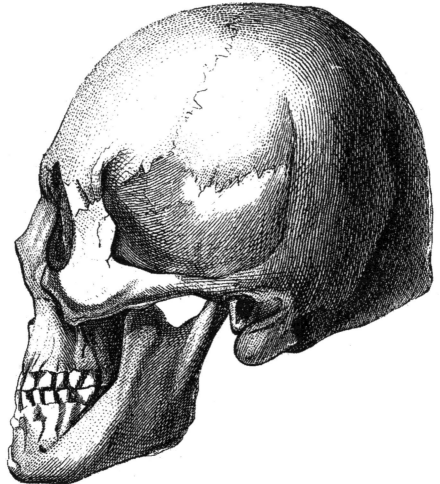

A12

A

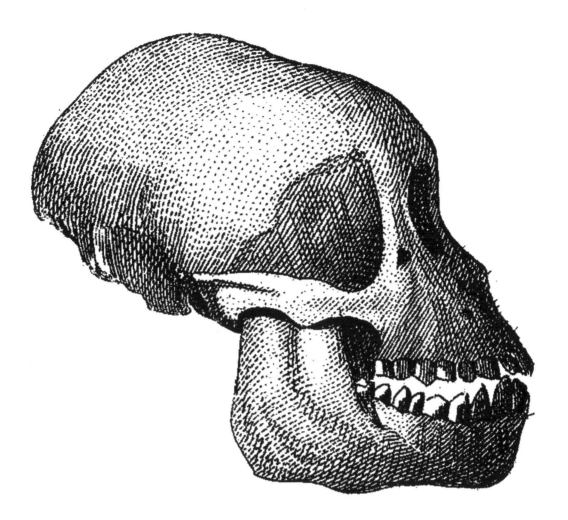

A13

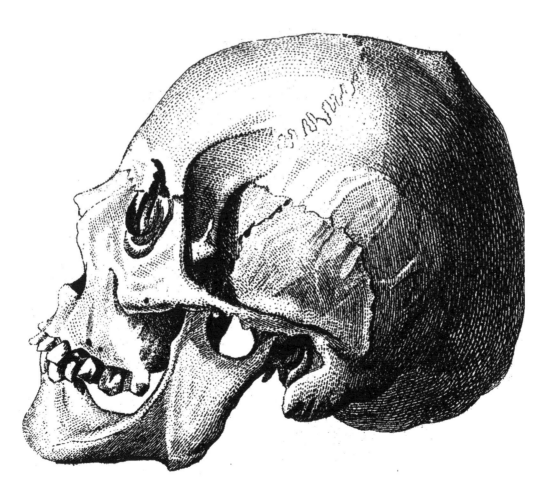

A14

A

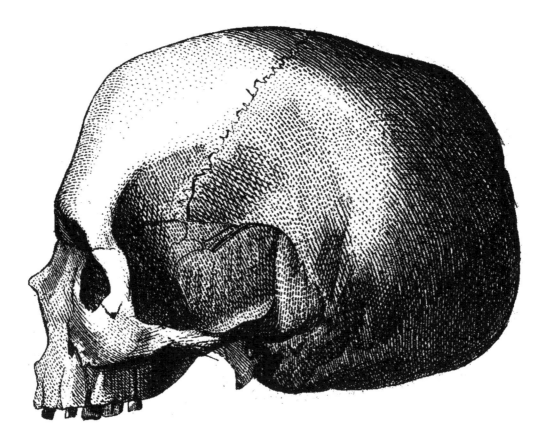

A15

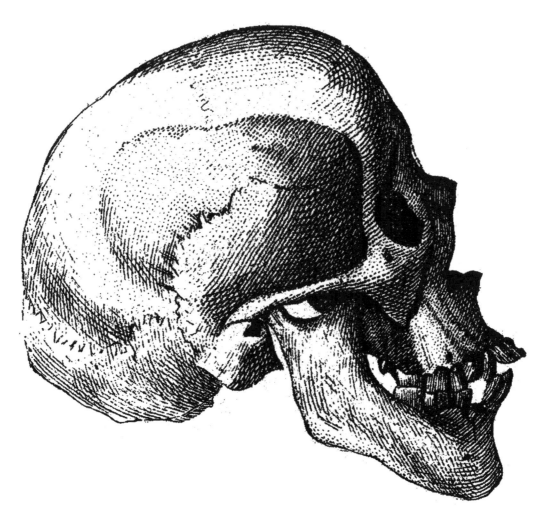

A16

A

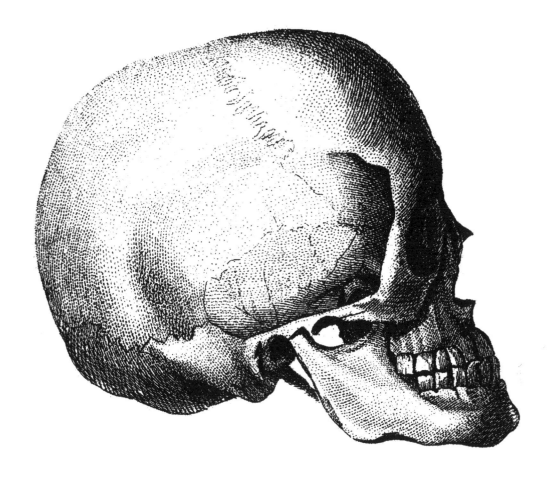

A17

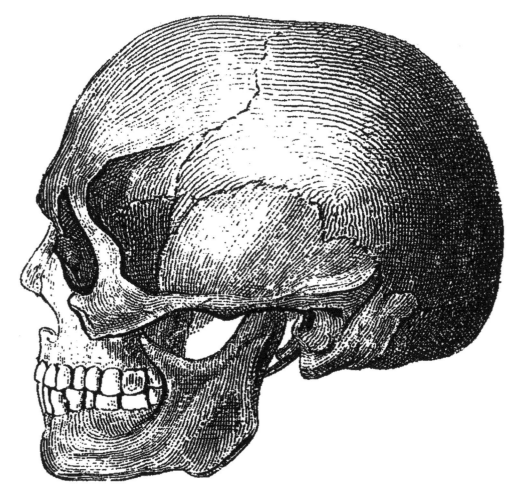

A18

A

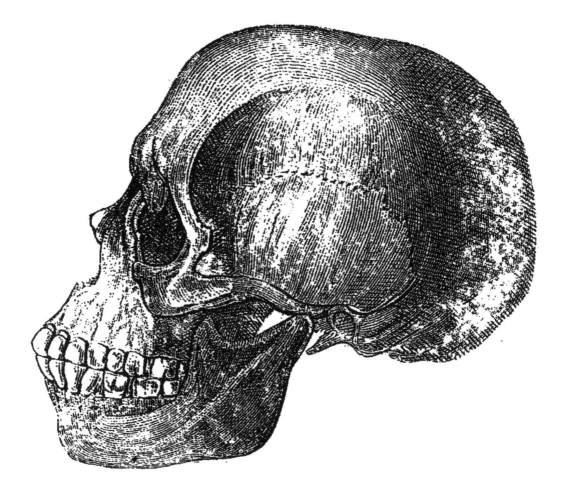

A19

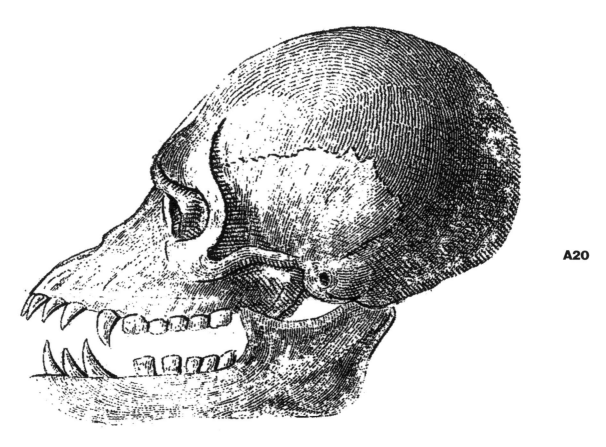

A20

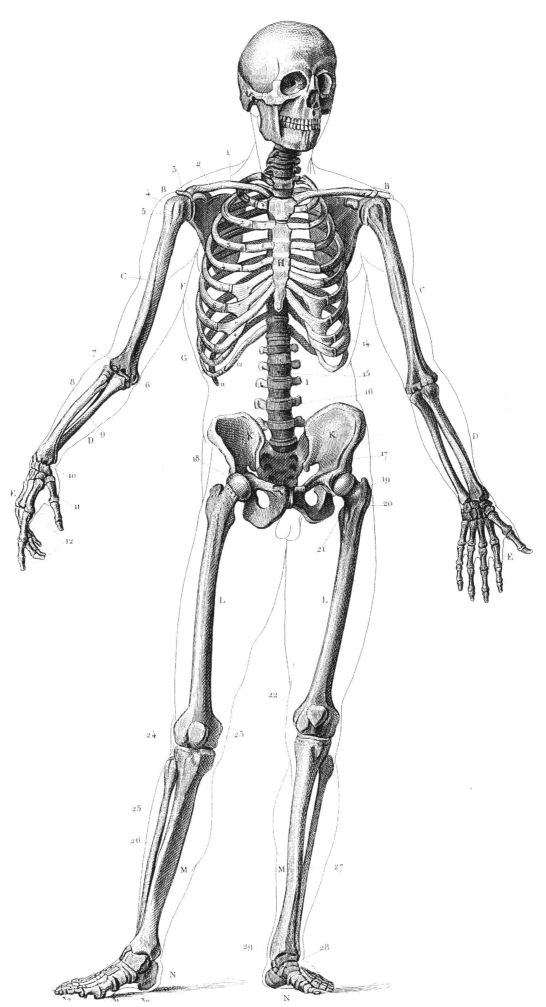

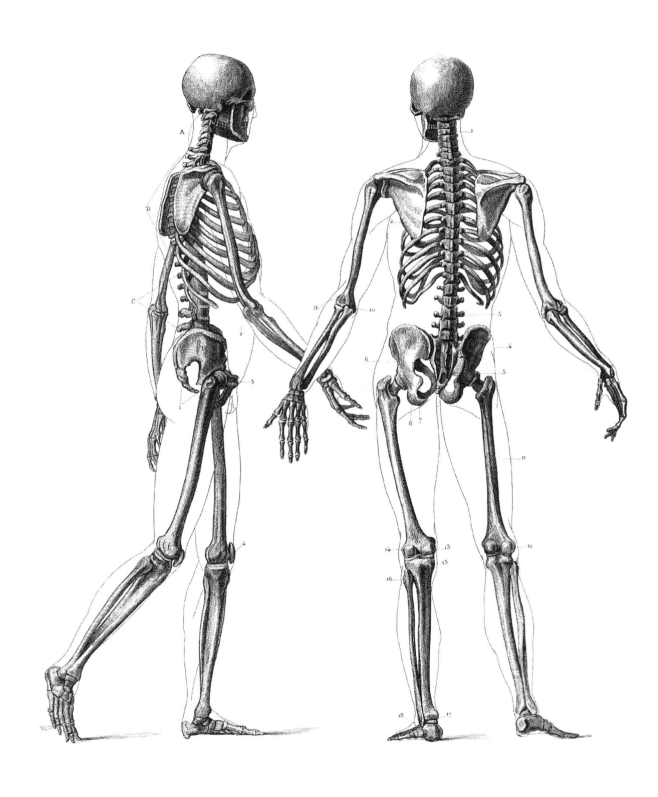

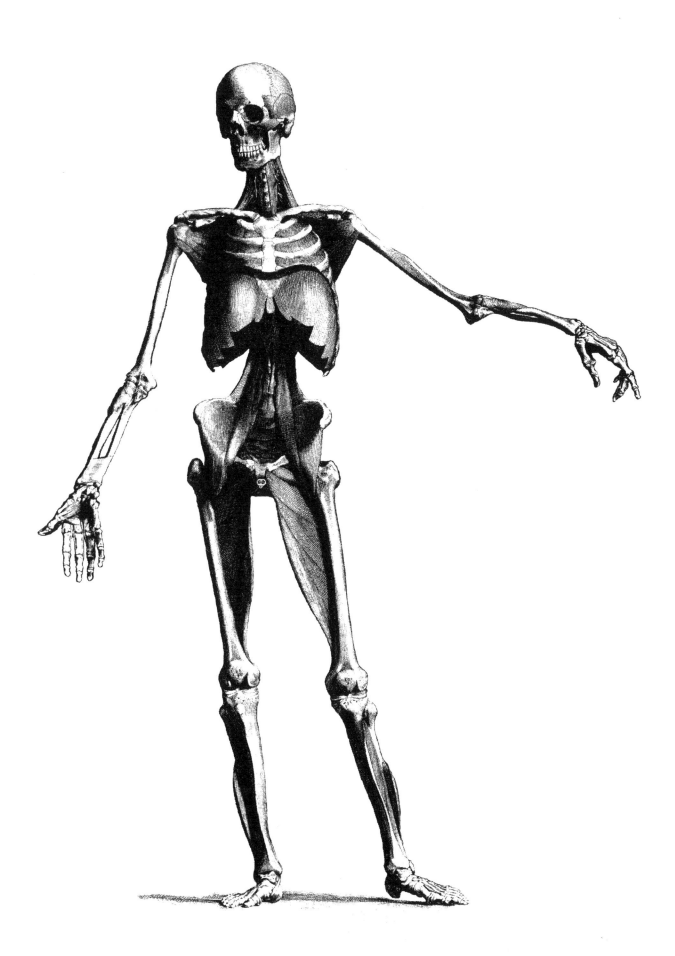

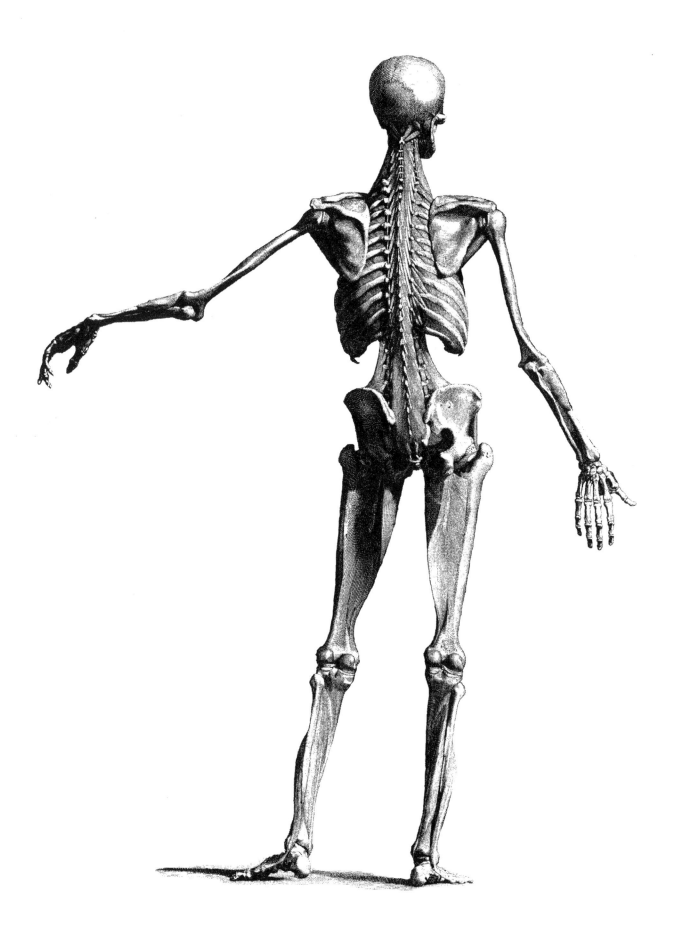

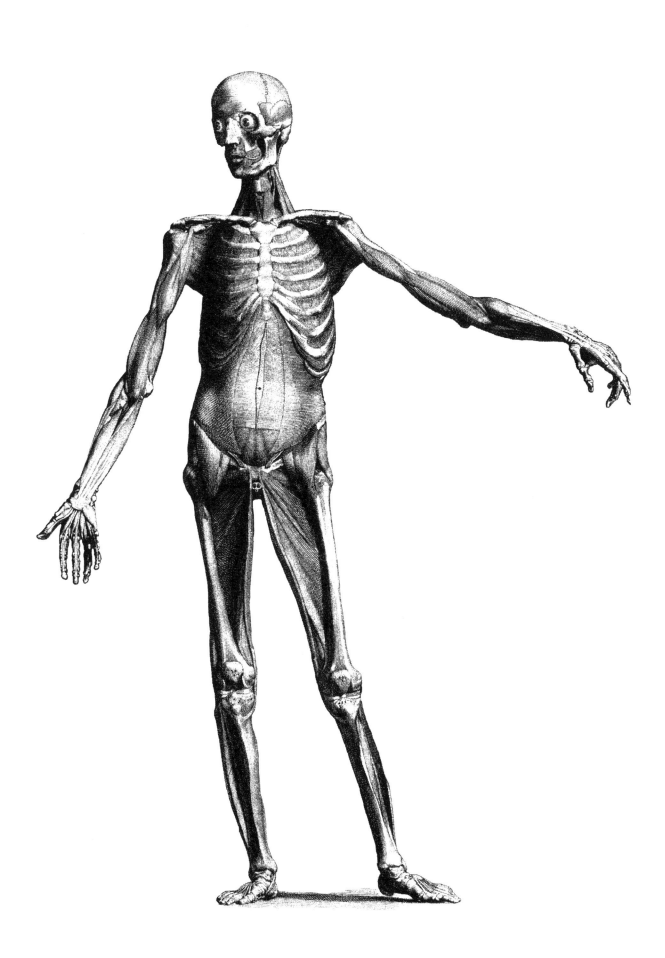

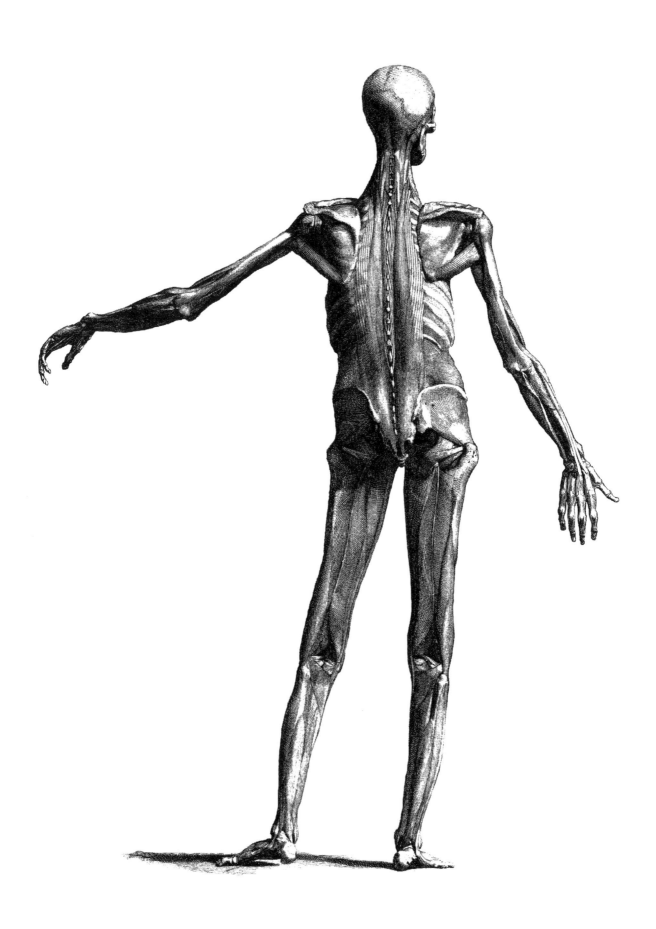

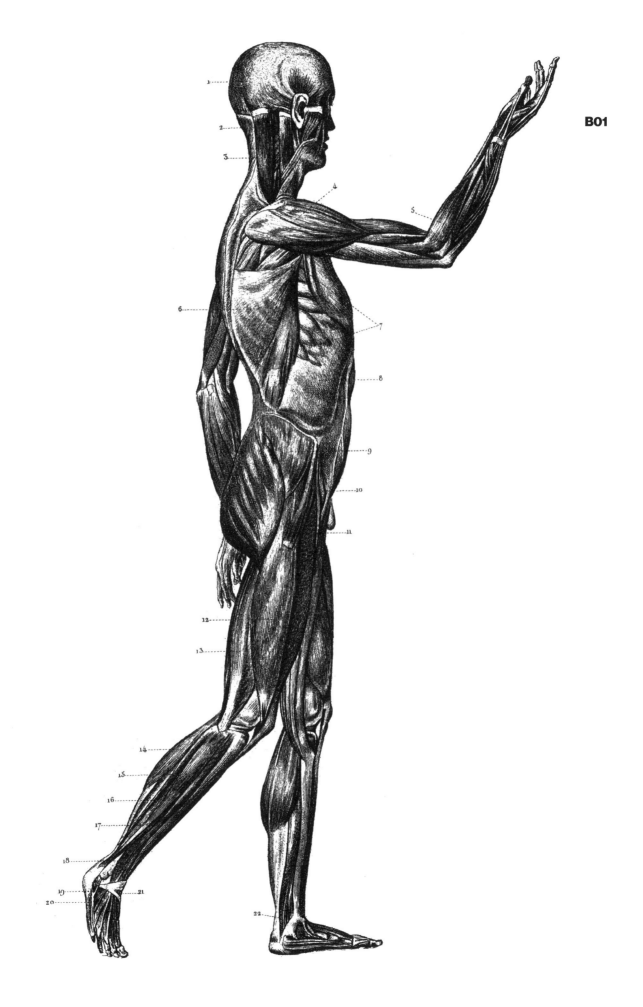

B01

B

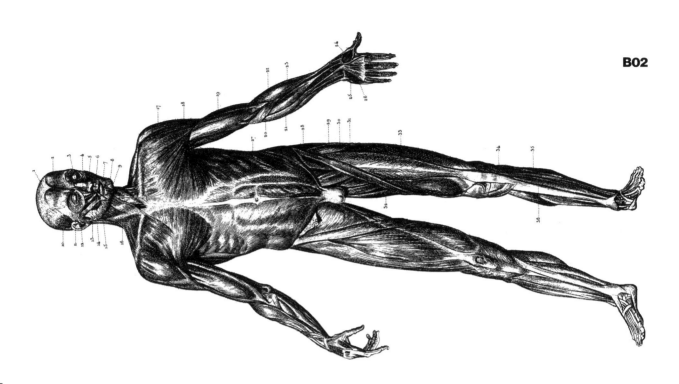

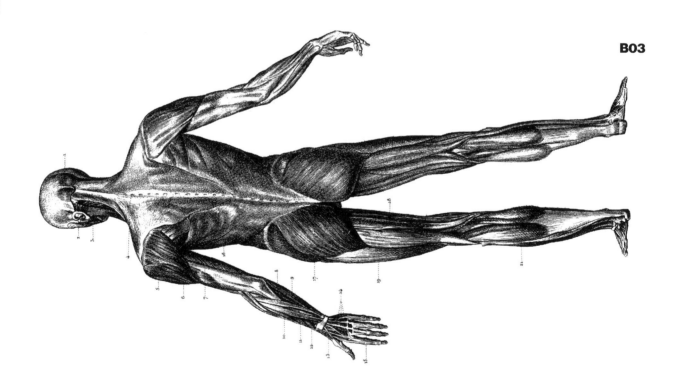

B

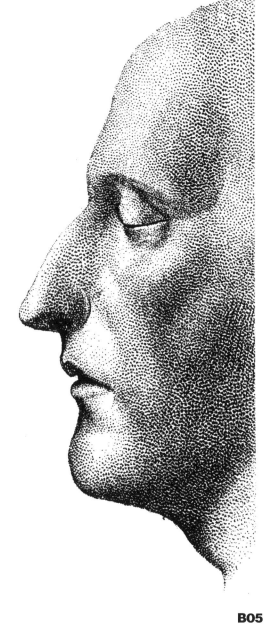

B04

B05

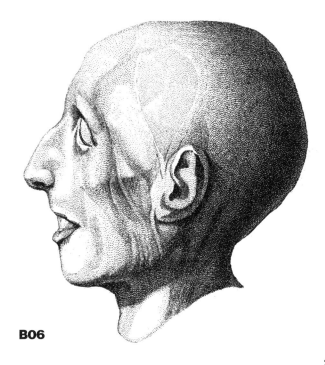

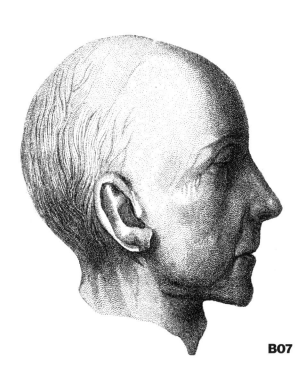

B06

B07

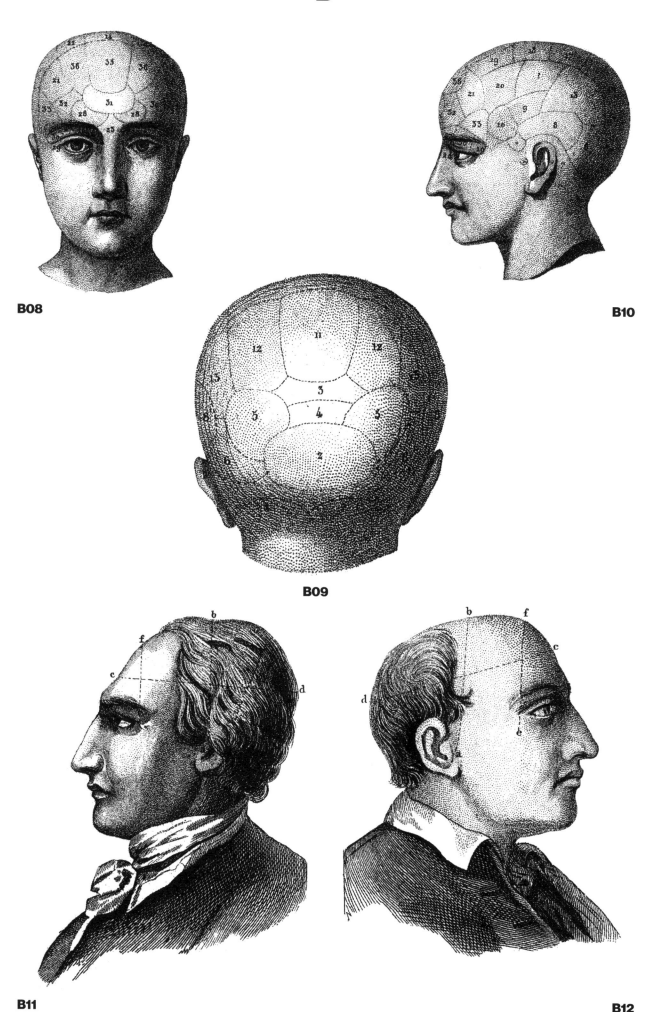

SKULLS & ANATOMY

B08

B10

B09

B11

B12

C

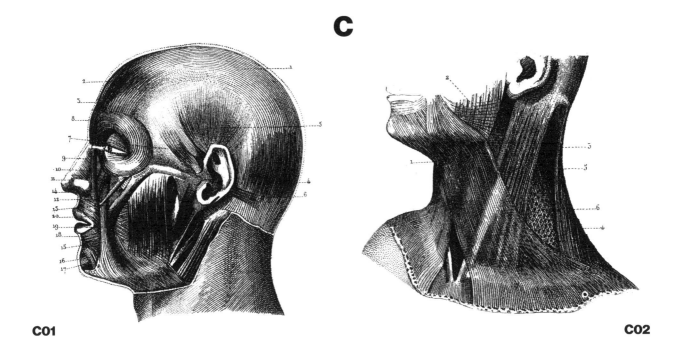

C01

C02

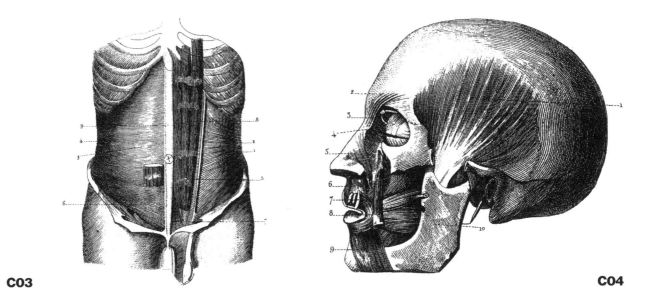

C03

C04

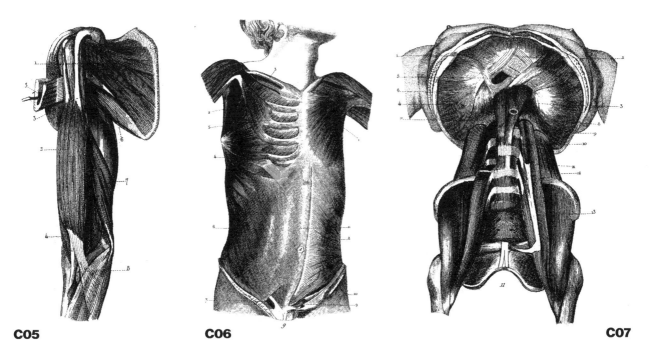

C05　　　　C06　　　　C07

C

C08

C09

C10

C

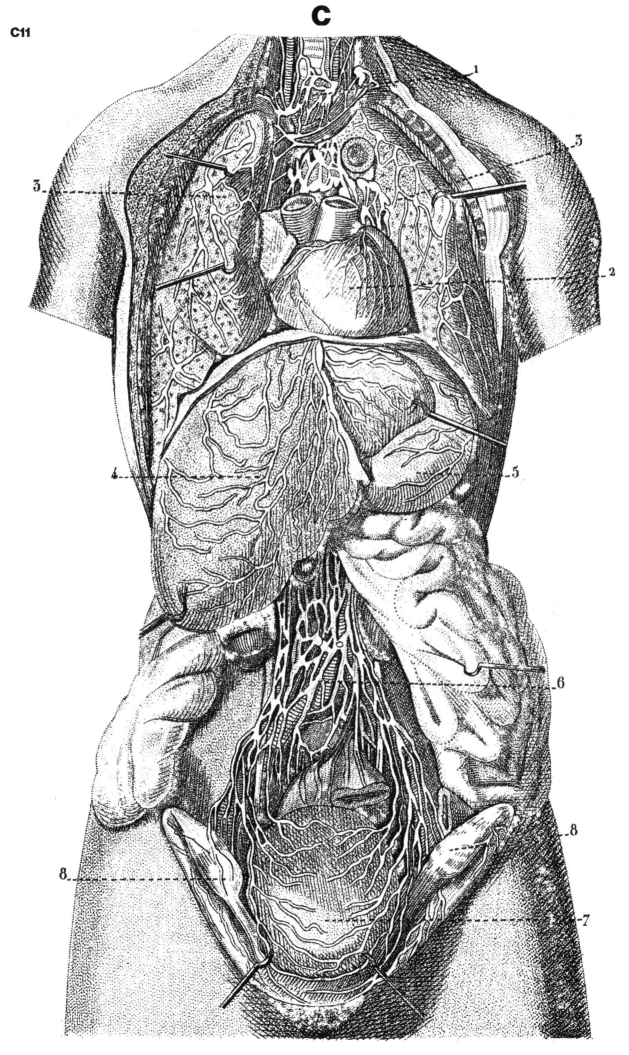

C

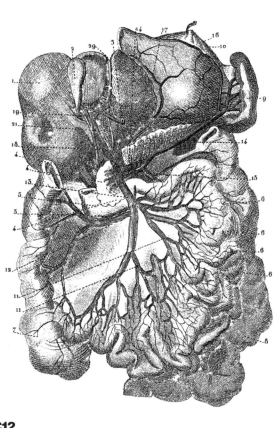

C12

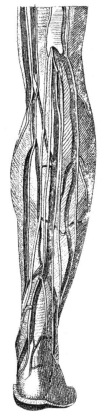

C13

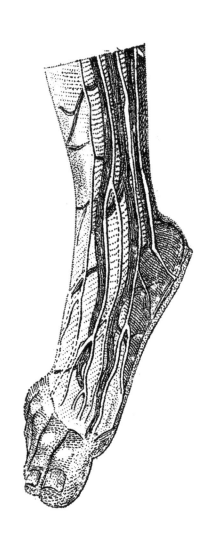

C14

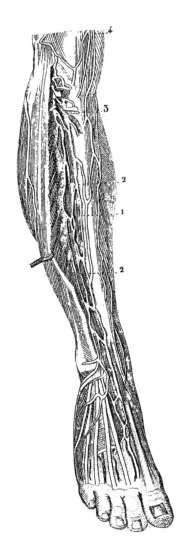

C15

C

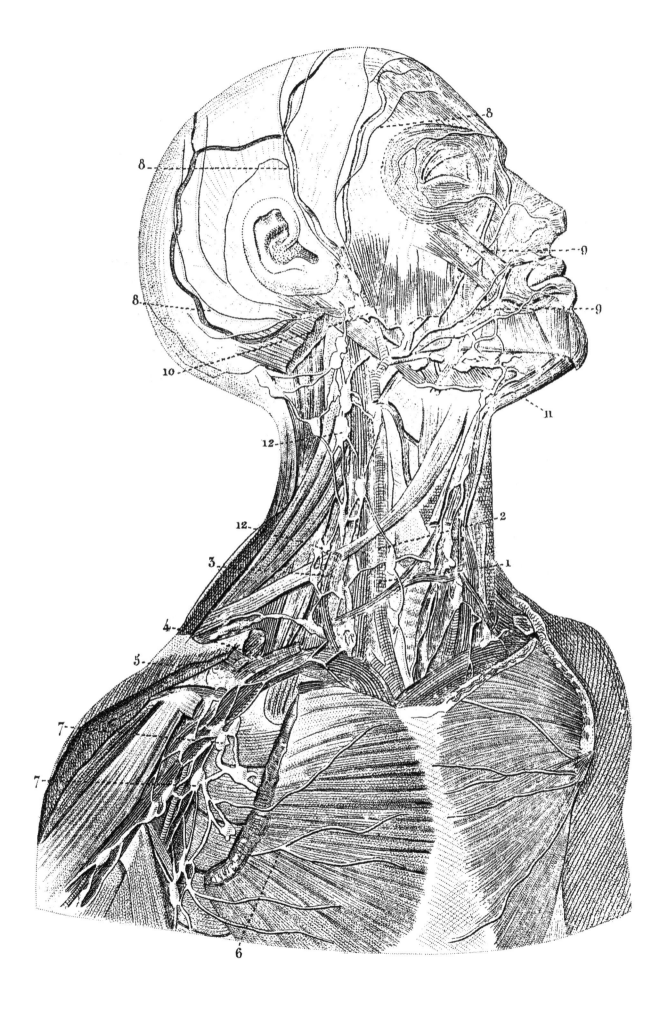

C

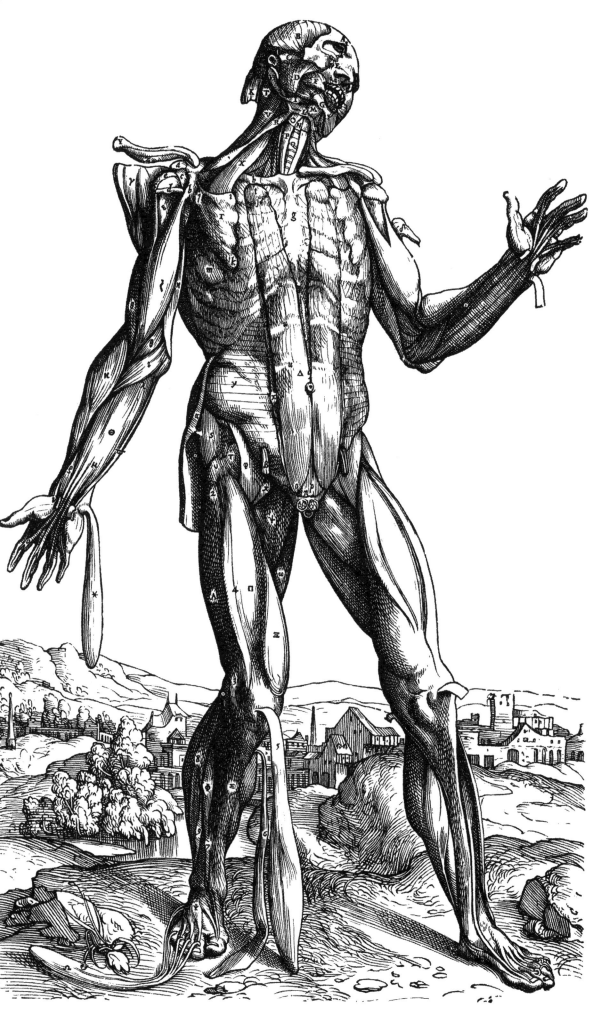

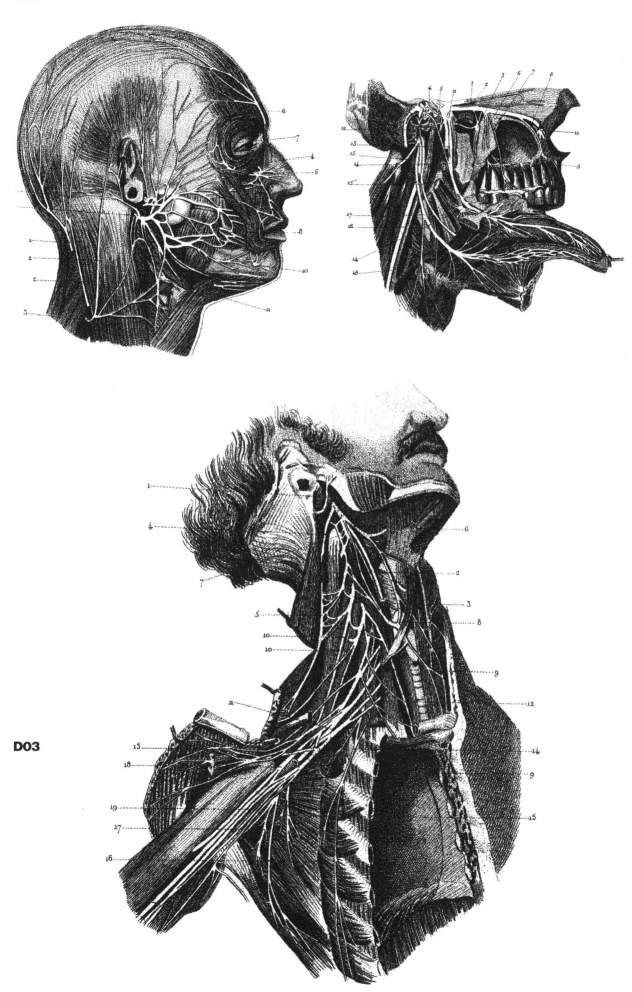

D06

D07

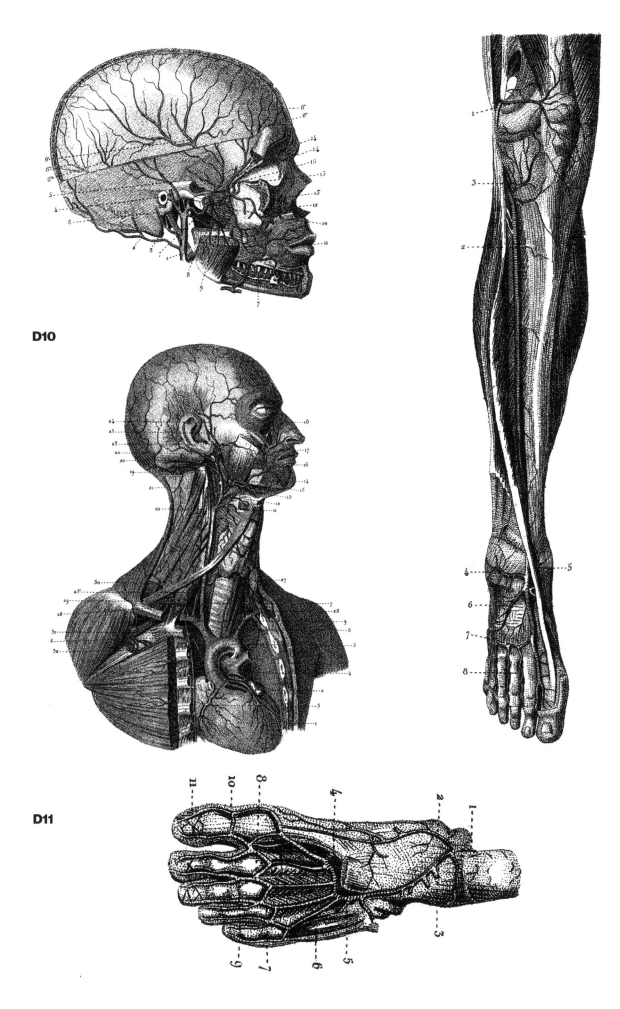

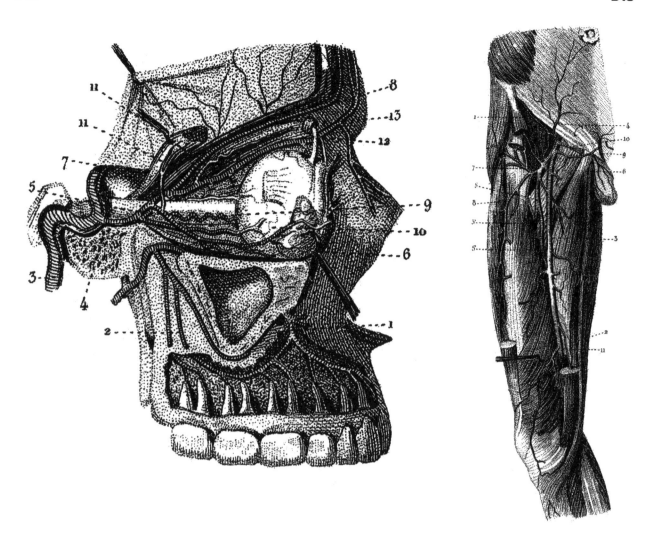

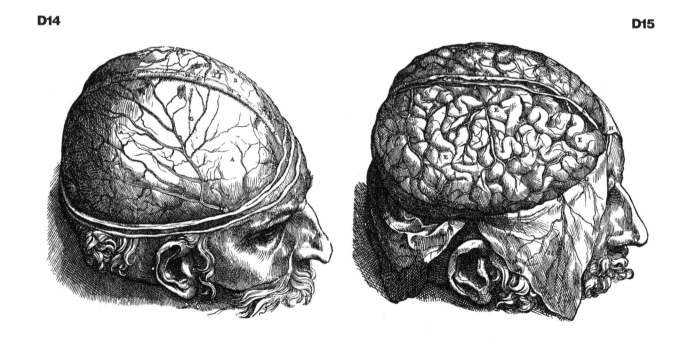

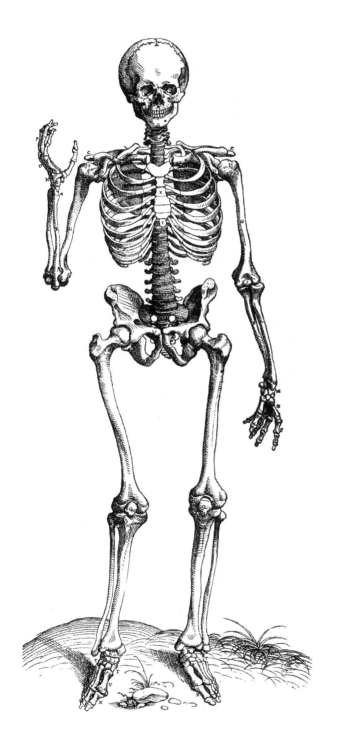

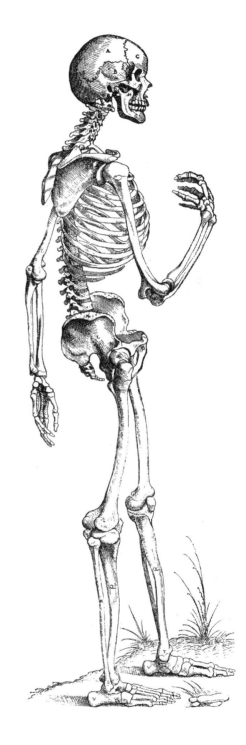

D18

D19

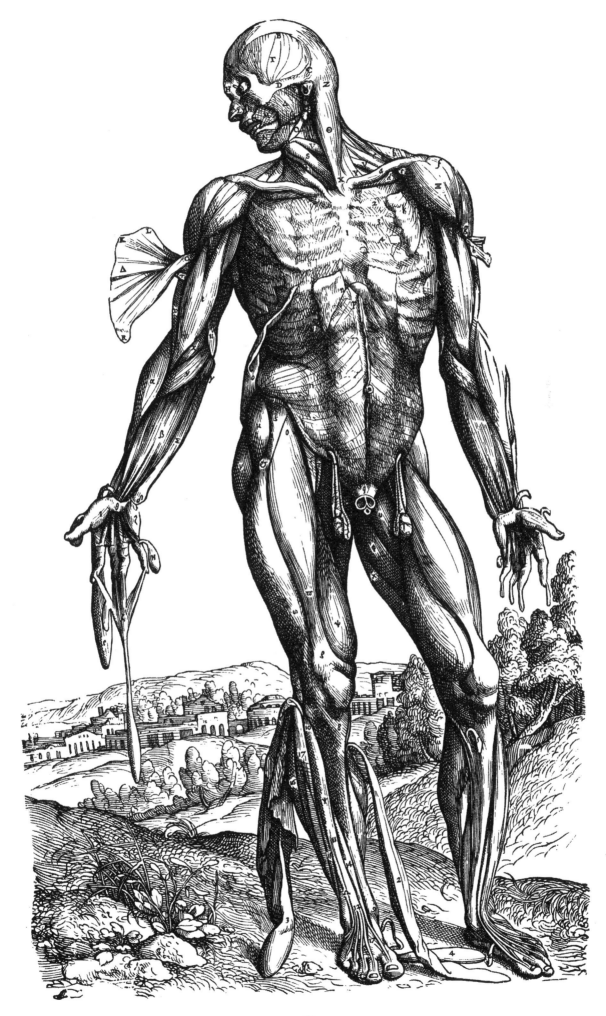

E01

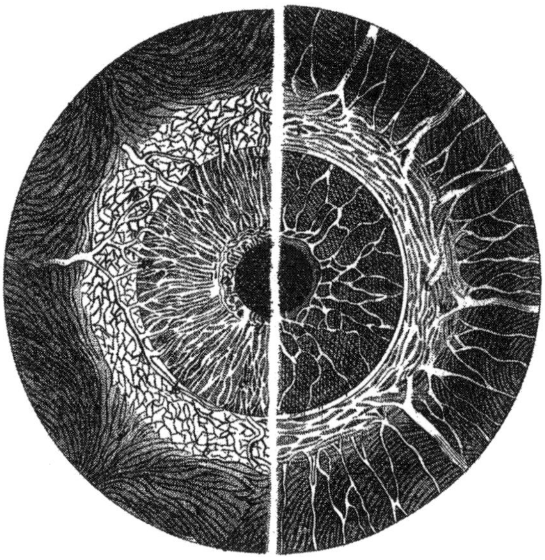

E02

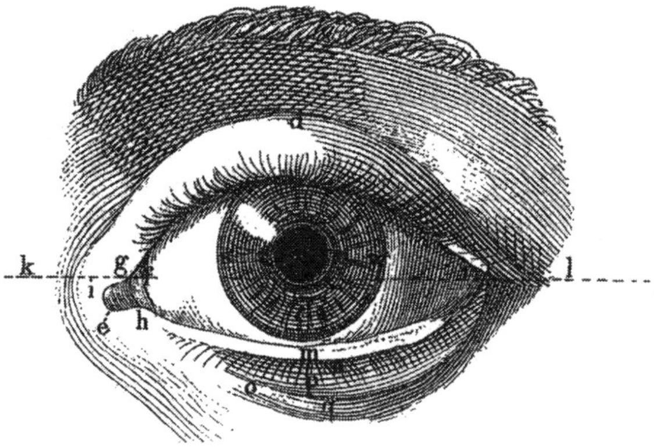

E03

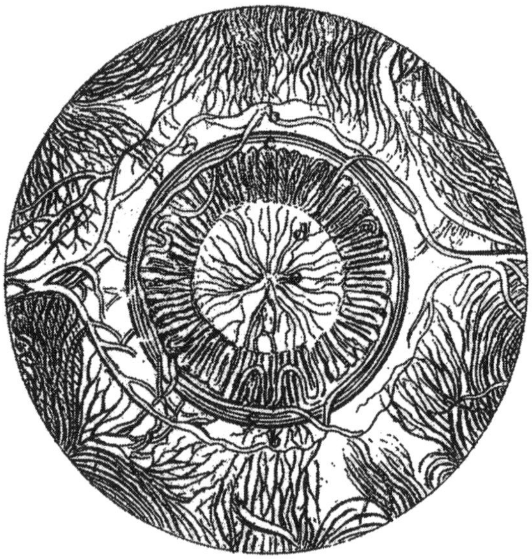

E04

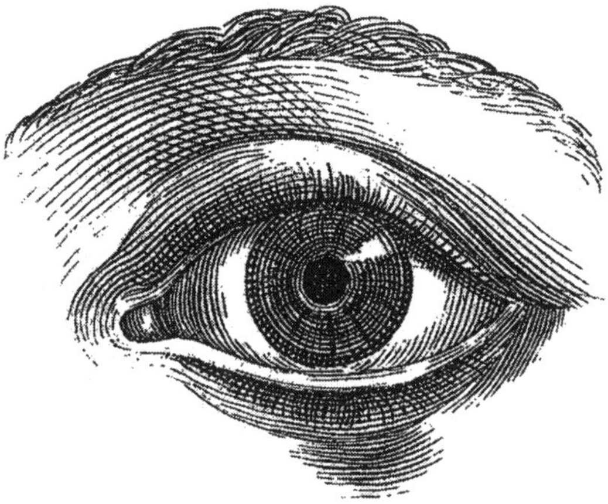

E05

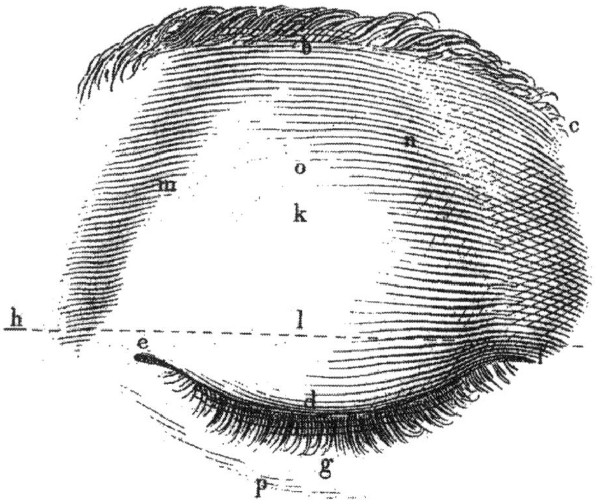

E06

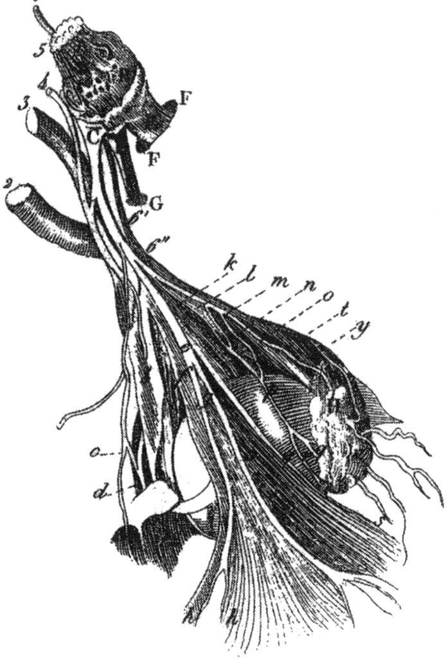

E07

E08

E09

E10

E11

E12

E13

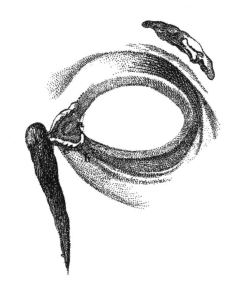

E14

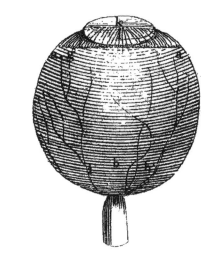

E15

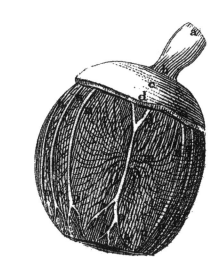

E16

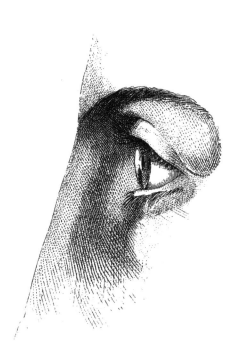

E17

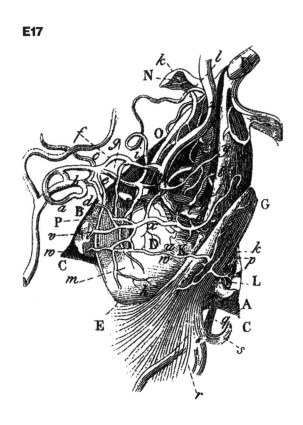

E18

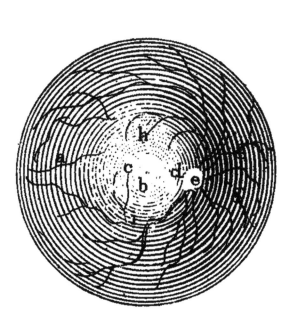

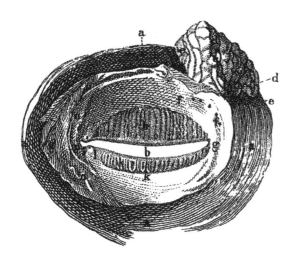

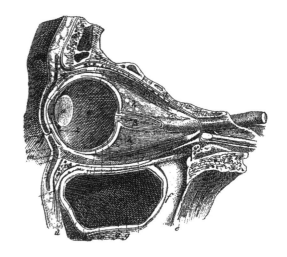

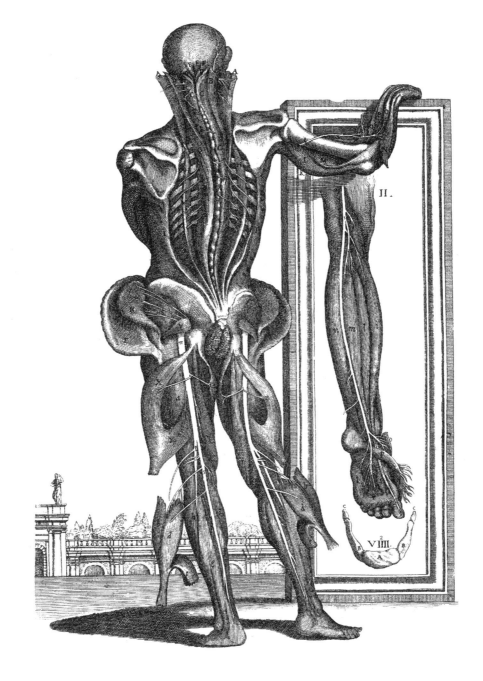

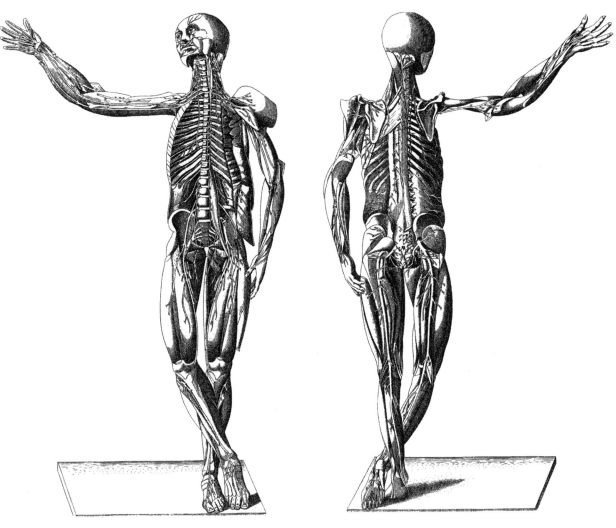

E24

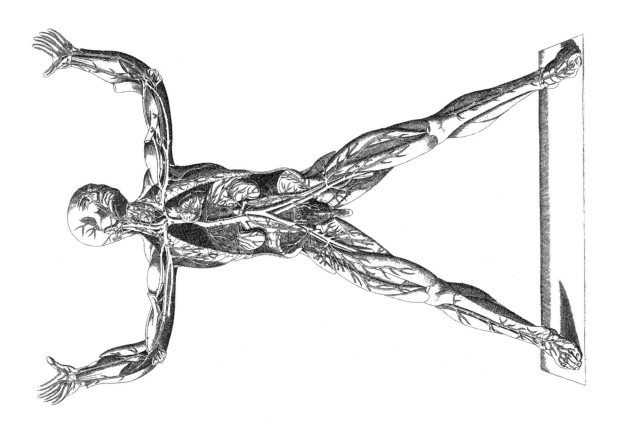

F01

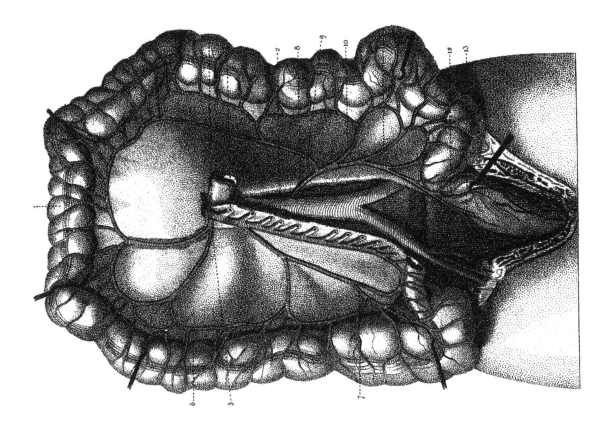

F02

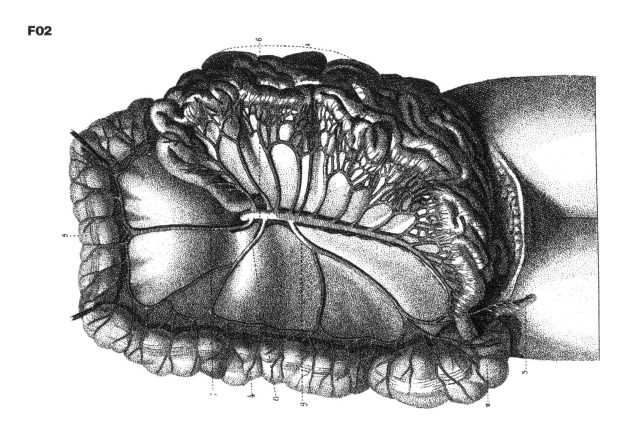

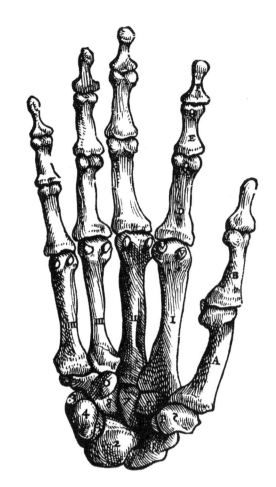

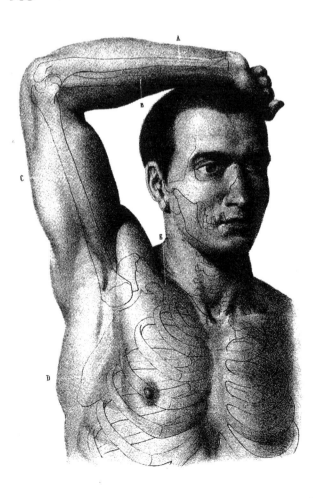

G

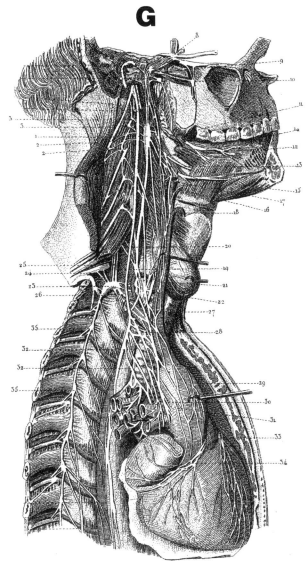

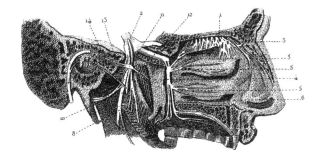

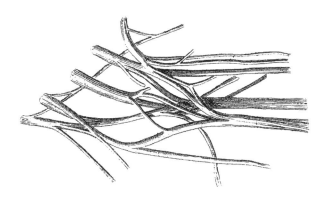

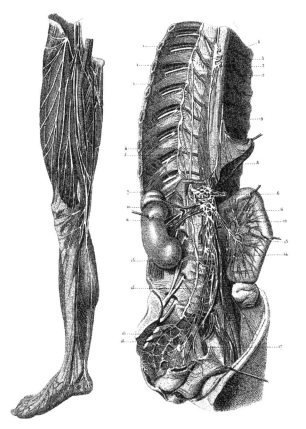

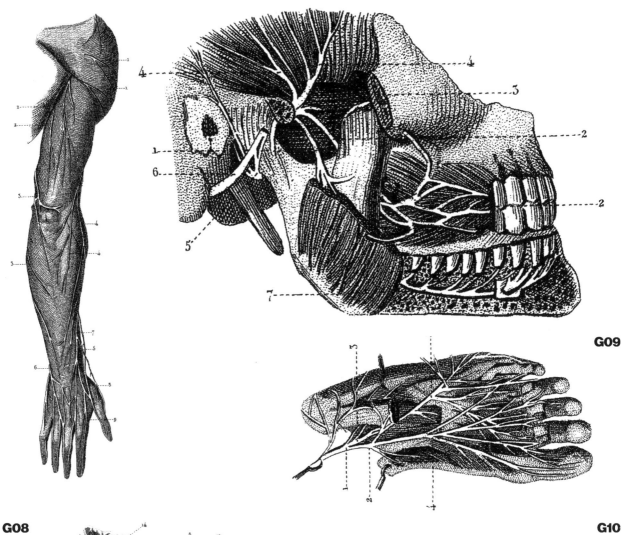

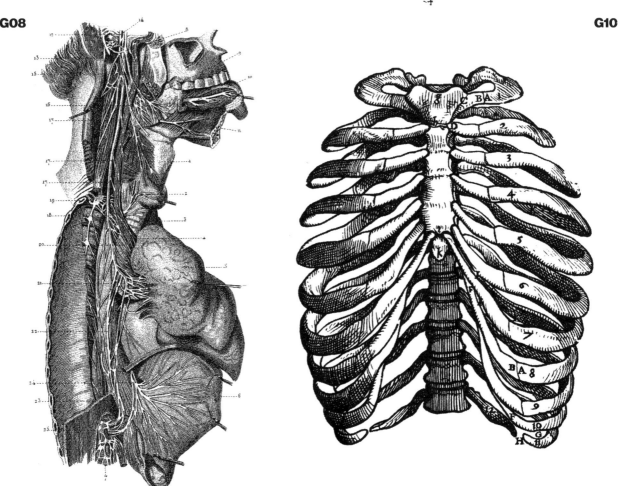

H01

H02

H03

H04

H05

H06

H07

H08

H09

H10

H11

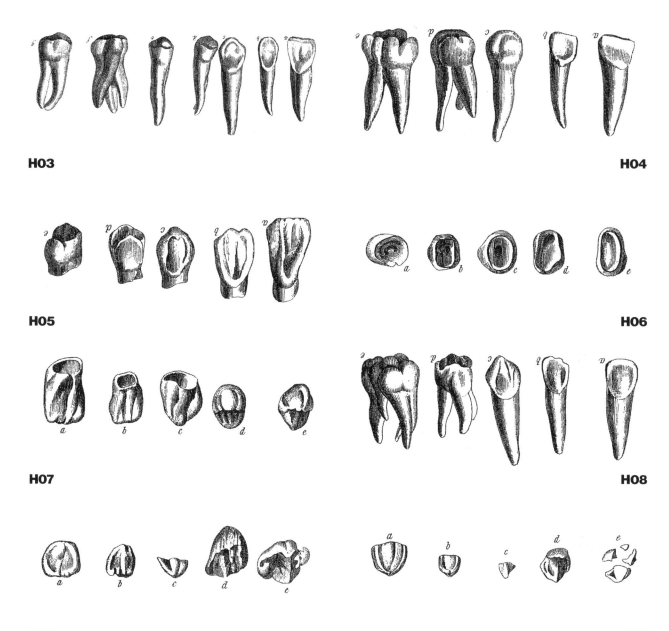

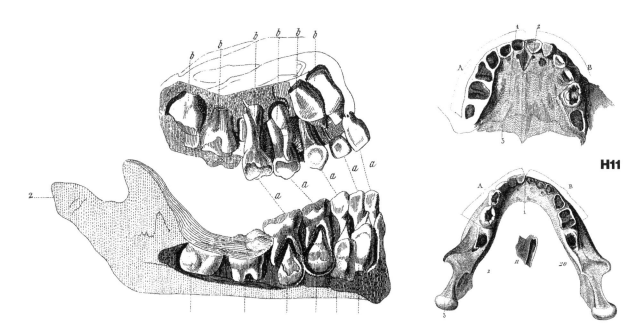

H12

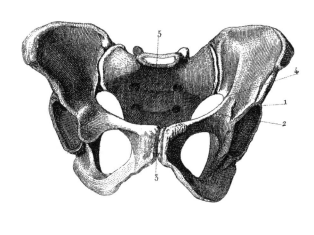

H13

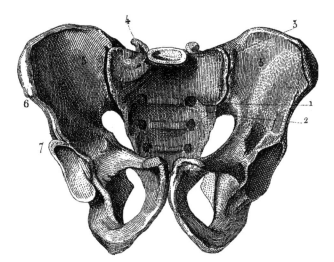

H14

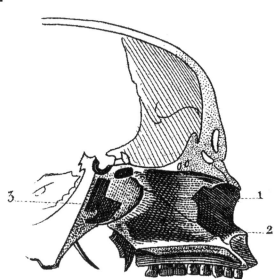

H15

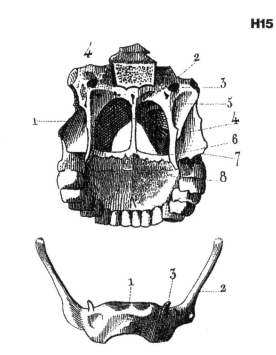

SKULLS & ANATOMY

H16

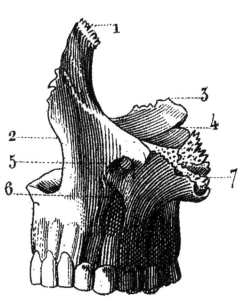

H17

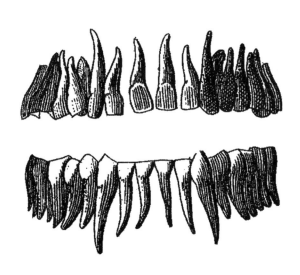

H18

H19

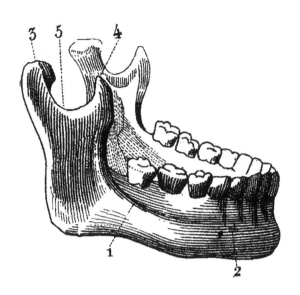

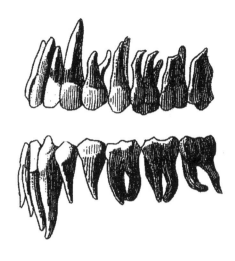

H20

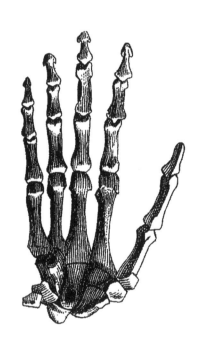

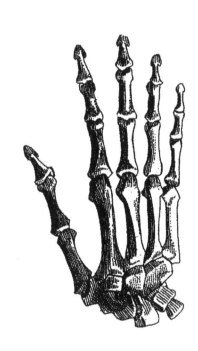

H21

101

102

103

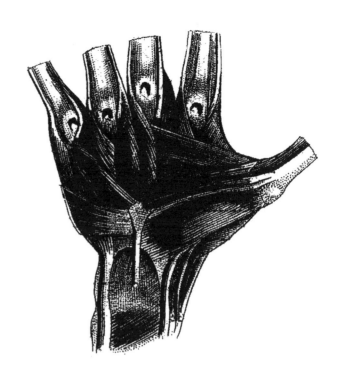

104

105

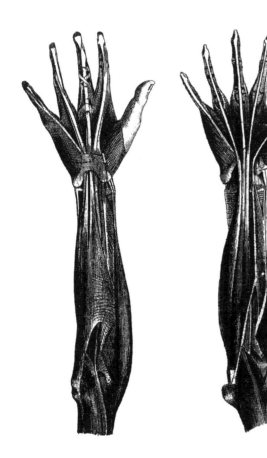

106

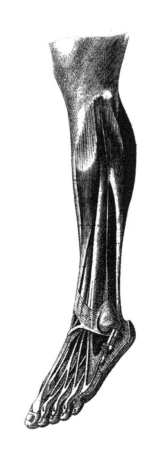

I

107

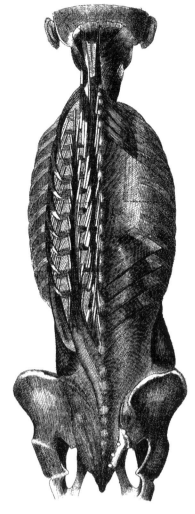

108

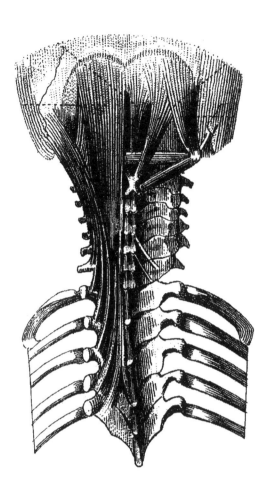

109

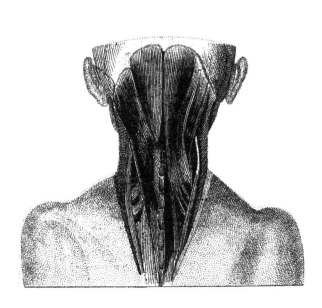

110

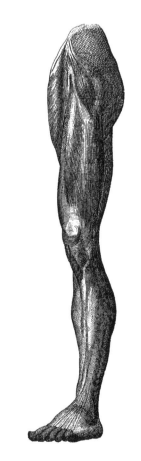

49

I11

I12

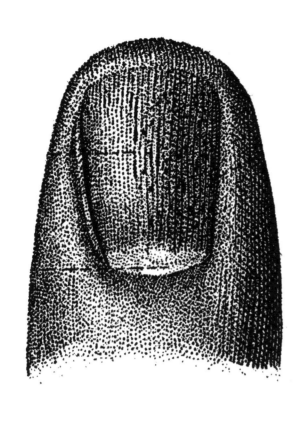

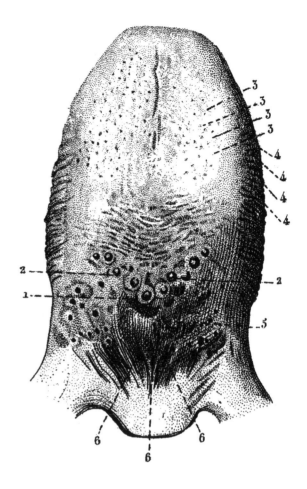

SKULLS & ANATOMY

I13

I14

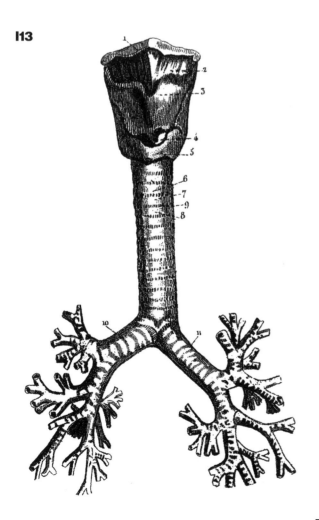

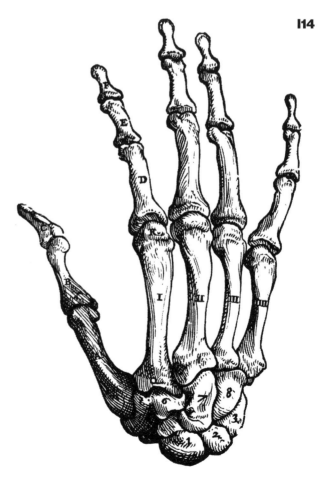

J01

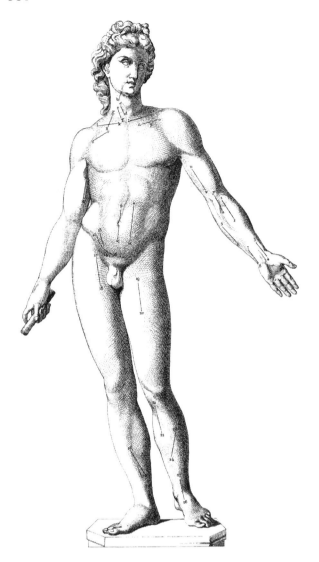

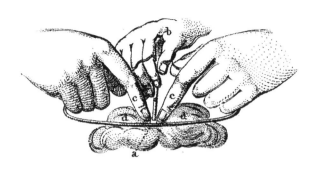

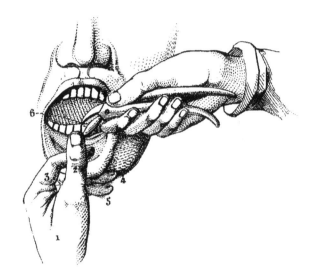

J04

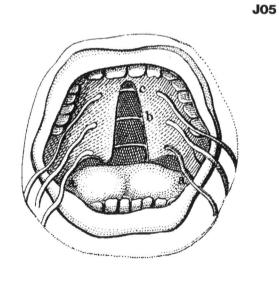

SKULLS & ANATOMY

J

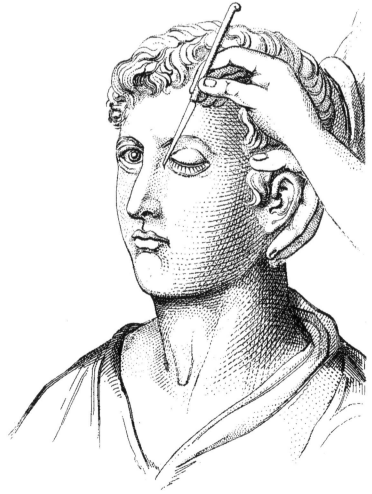

J

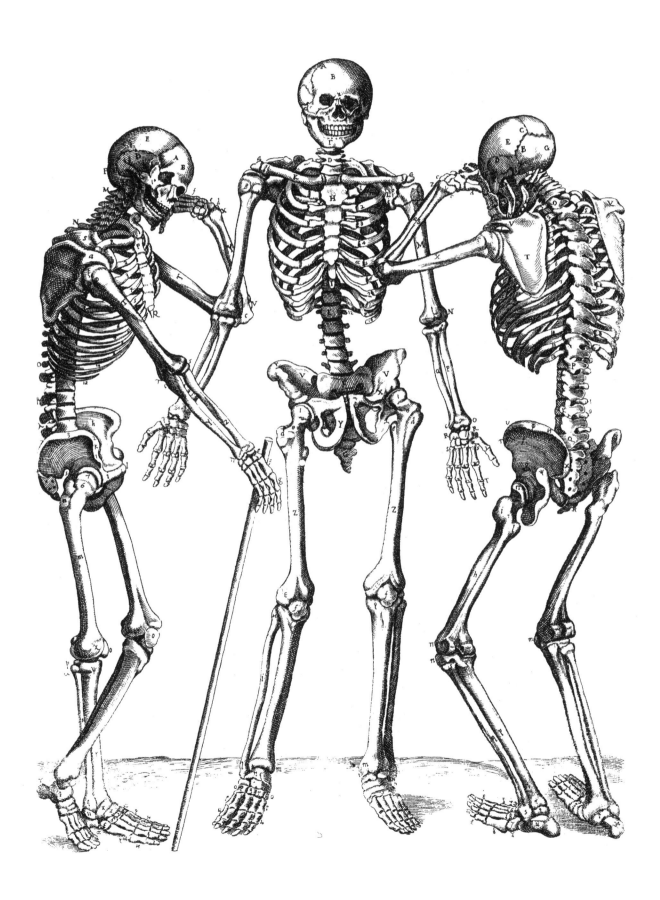

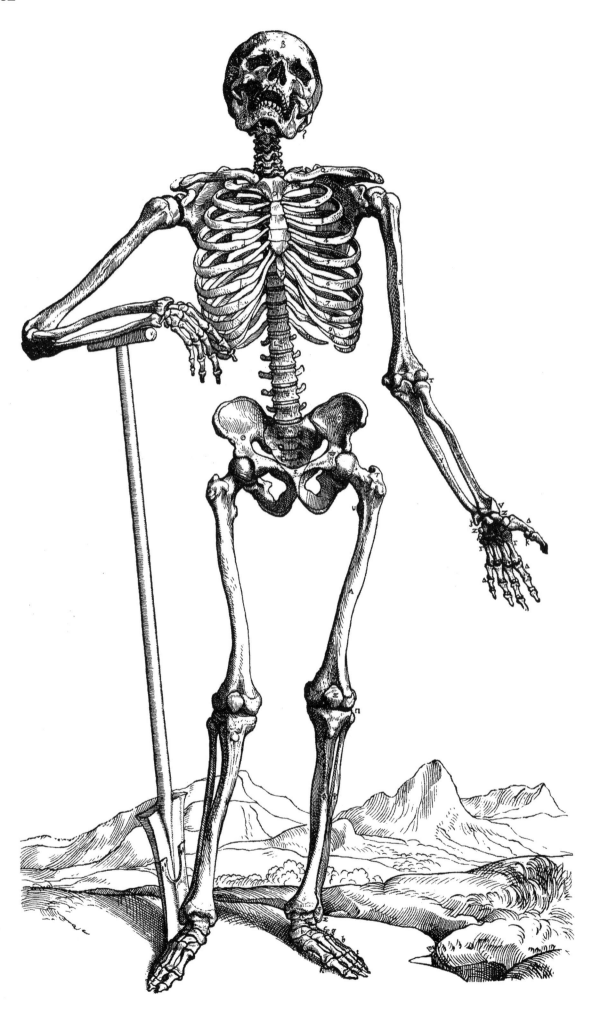

K03

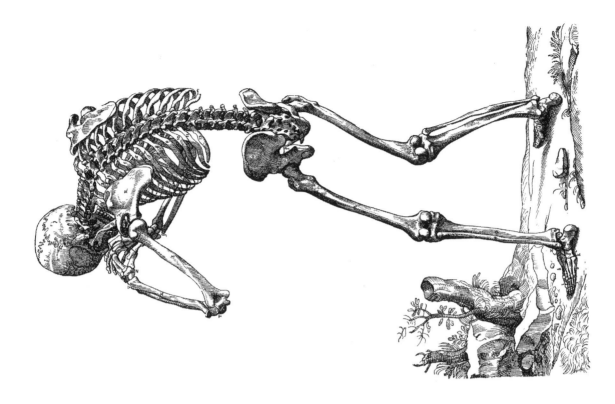

K04

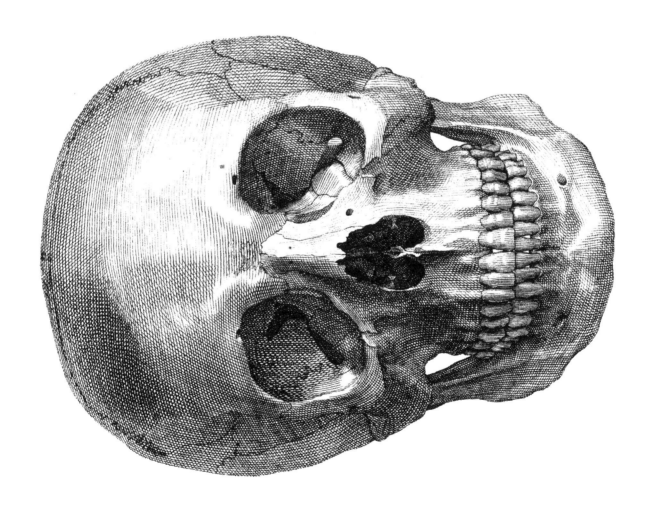

SKULLS & ANATOMY

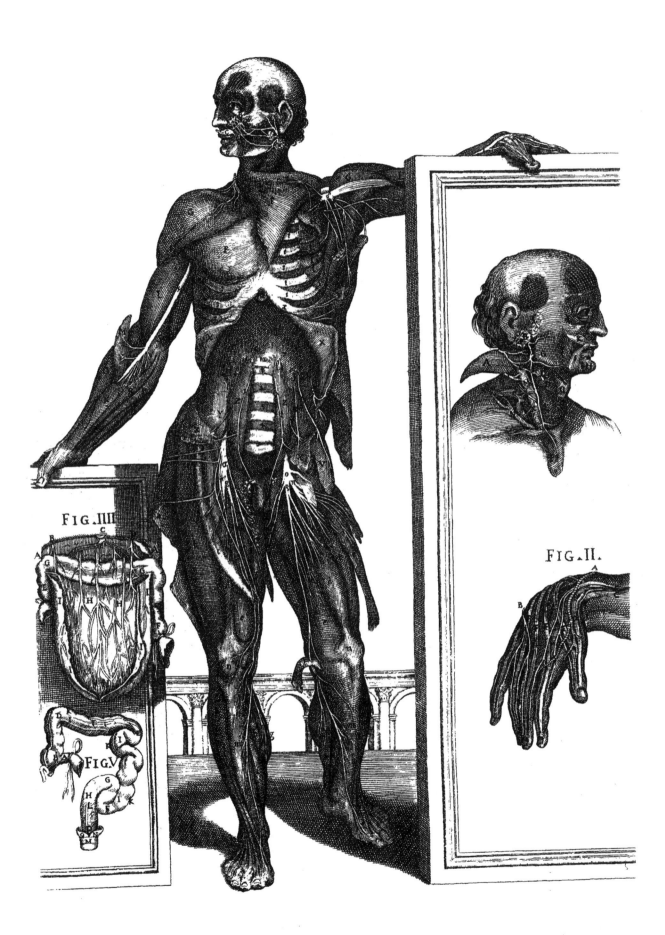

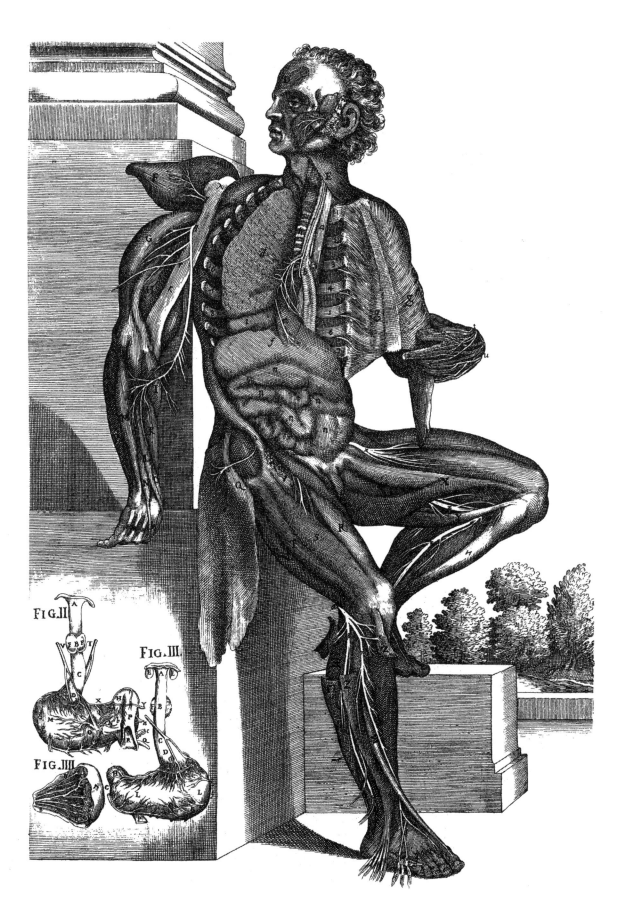

FIG.II.

FIG.III.

FIG.IIII.

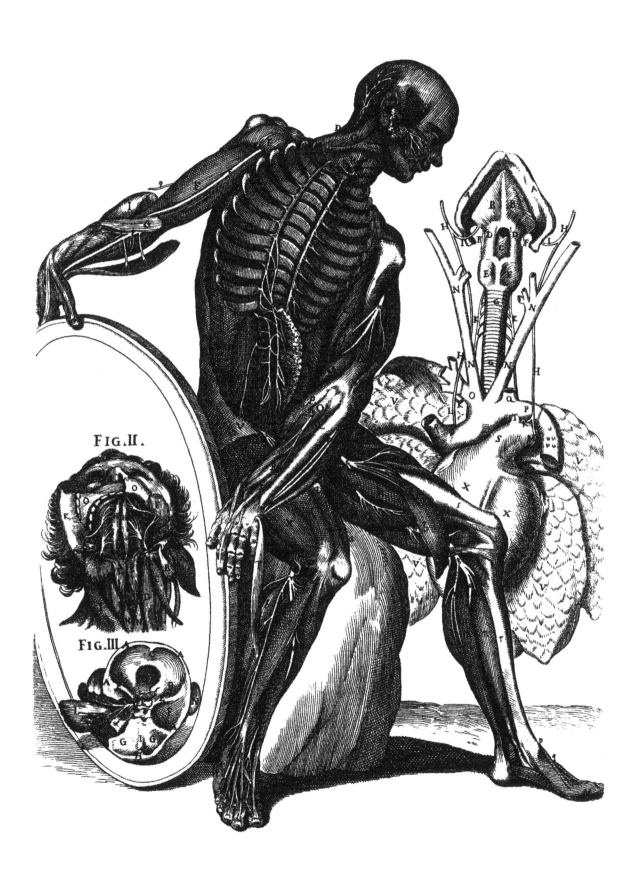

FIG.II.

FIG.III.

L

L01

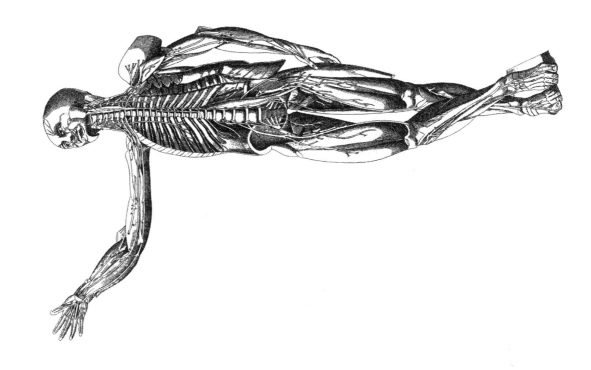

L02

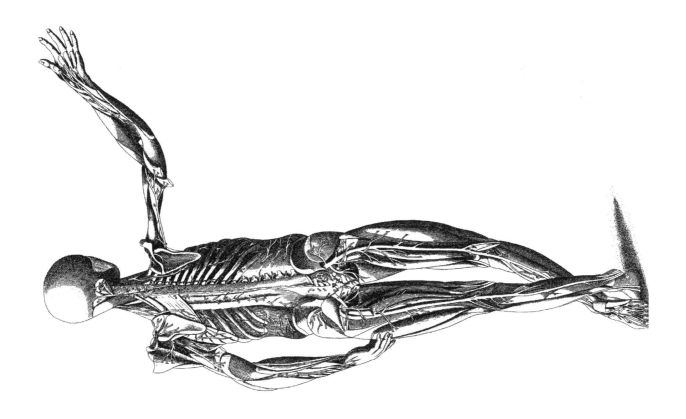

L03

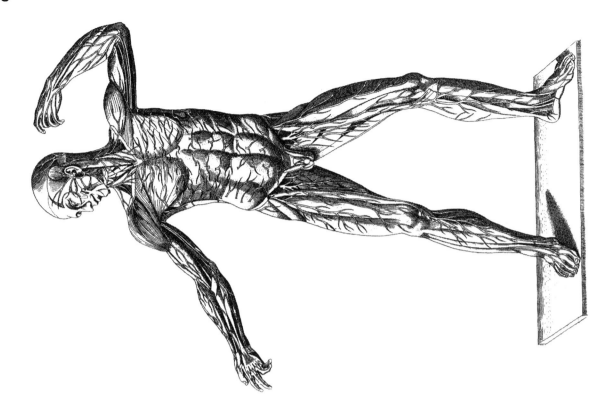

L04

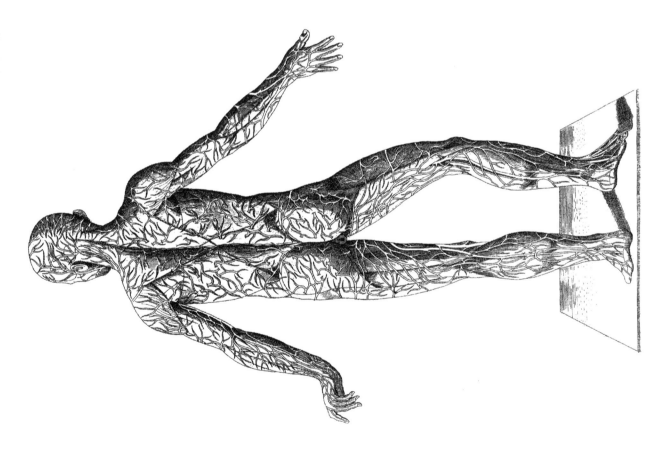

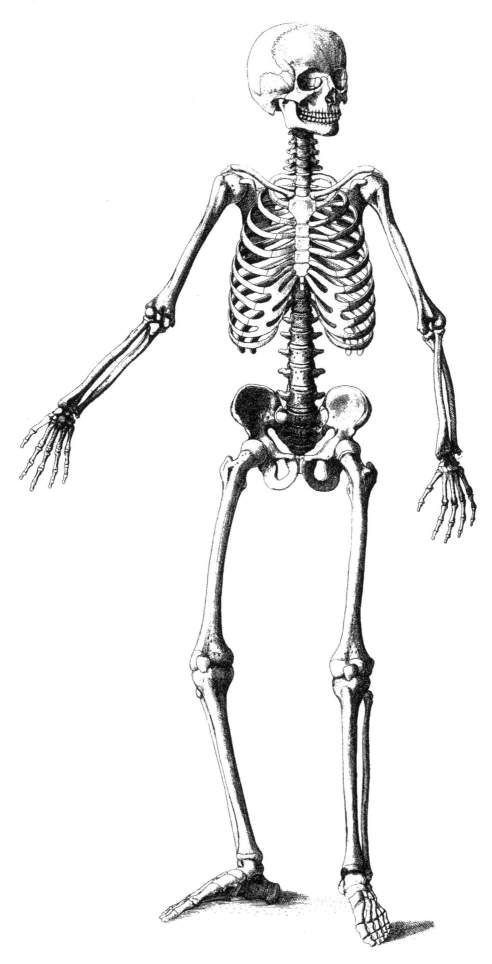

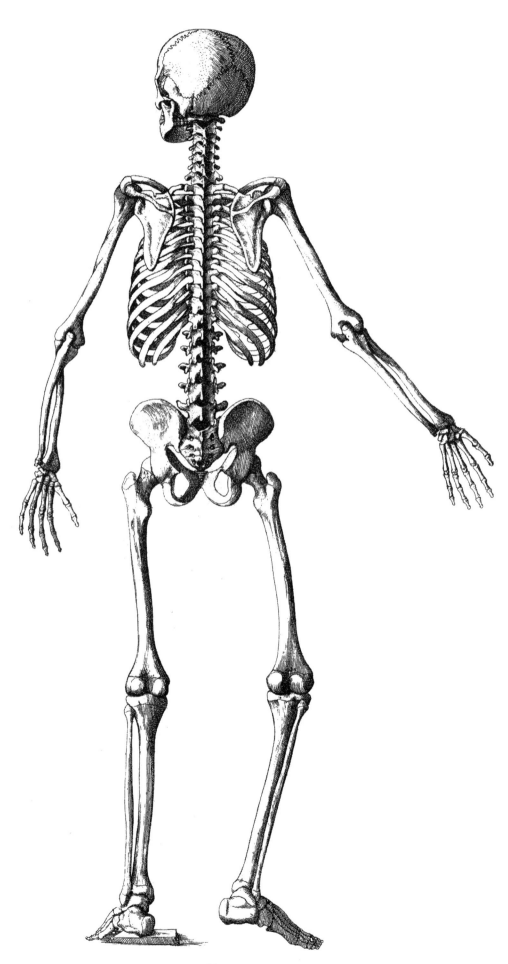

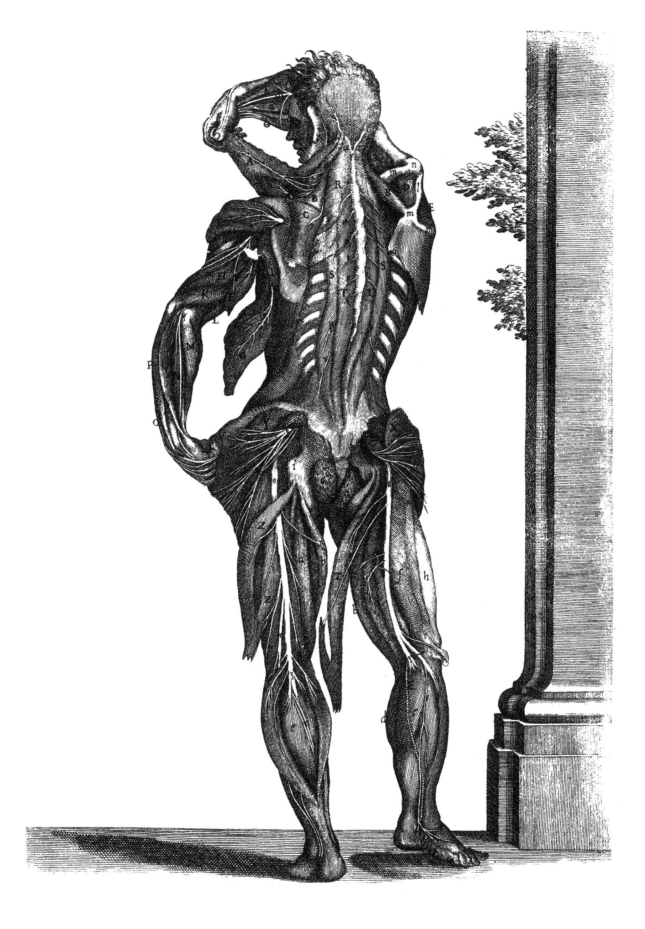

SKULLS & ANATOMY

COPYRIGHT FREE VINTAGE ILLUSTRATIONS FOR ARTISTS AND DESIGNERS

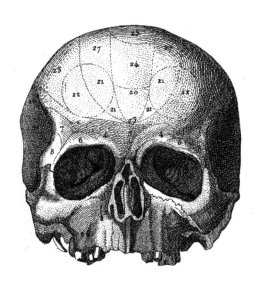

VAULTEDITIONS.COM

Printed in Great Britain
by Amazon